The Aspens and Whatnot

The Aspens and Whatnot

Poems by Donald Gasperson

Goldfish Press
Seattle

Goldfish Press
4545 42nd Avenue Southwest
Suite 211
Seattle, WA 98116-4243

Manufactured in the United States of America

ISBN-13: 978-1-950276-13-4

Library of Congress Control Number 2020952962

Many of these poems were published in the following journals:

Better than Starbucks, Big Window Review, The Remembered Arts.
W.I.N.K, Poetry Pacific, Vox Poetica, Quail Bell Magazine,
The Bitchin' Kitsch, Foliate Oak Literary Review, Futures Trading
Literature, Five Willows Literary Review, Doubly Mad,
Chrysanthemum Literary Anthology

Book and cover design by Koon Woon

Contents

The Aspens

standing in the glacial till
where the river rocks drift
along the slow seasons

illuminated by vine and leaf
consecrated of root and berry
practicing mindfulness again

and after hard years of becoming
there's a sad feeling of being
simply awkward and old

but the communion with silence
evokes the quietest of sounds
touchingly and achingly clear

the linen white boles of aspens
spring green leaves
trembling

no title

a butterfly flutters by
elegant as a breeze
light as sunshine

The Tide

Stirring up a fire
in the chill half-light
a watercolor sunrise

Leaving a path in the dew
at this juncture
of the sun and moon

Following the tide tables
onto the reach
of a broad flat beach

The tired waves
rolling back on themselves
toward the wide horizon

Past the deep tidal pools
where in isolated spots
there are caves in the rock

That when visible
harbor in themselves
a quiet urgency

Icicle Creek

Leaving town at last
and running for the pass,
the radio ringing out
my rock and roll past.

Forest service dust,
gravel, rattling travel
and ragged, high desert heat,
rolling all the windows down.

Even sturdy antelope,
those sage brush saints,
can't thrive long
on flat, iron mirages.

But around an outcrop
there's a palpable peace,
at the tar and timber bridge
over Icicle Creek.

I stop and walk about,
looking forward
to the next twenty miles
of ruts and potholes.

The stream's generous with time,
forever entering on the moment,

sunlight and shadow,
time, and possible grace.

There's a small camp,
undeveloped and undiscovered.
I arrived here this evening
coming to a full stop.

With space for my meager needs
and a blackened fire-pit,
I open my pack, surprised
it's full of sentiment.

Quiet as the twilight,
I put together a fire,
it's odd brewing tea
in all these memories.

But there's a bend in the stream
where driftwood washes up,
so, I wished myself here
at Icicle Creek.

.

Barefoot

the buddha
flagrant in his transparency

was motivation and motion
for those with sensible shoes

but being barefoot
quiets the idle mind

and mindfulness
is a simple thing

The Silver Surf Motel

Driving, tired and anxious,
spiraling down the coast,
my ass wired to the road.

But rolling to a stop
and collecting memories
at the Silver Surf Motel.

Silver as driftwood
washed up on the shore
and lodging there.

It's serendipity,
and the proprietor agrees,
handing us the keys.

Ann agrees,
"it's a lucky find,"
and on that we all agree.

But attending to the room
and the sound of the ocean,
we both grow older.

I'm still restless enough,
with the evening rolling in,
to walk down to the beach.

Ann's tired and it's cold out.
but I invite her for a walk.
"I know you're fond of me,"

"But no thanks, Don
and it's 'I love you,'"
looking through the delivery menu.

Satisfied, I walk loose jointed
and shambling a little
onto the face of the beach.

Mindfully, it's a tough time,
flirting with anxiety
and a studied peace.

Trying to find some assurance
in the relentless twilight
of my life.

But soaking up the big empty
to the hollow sound
of my world on fire.

And finding that after-life insurance,
with preexisting conditions,

has outrageous premiums.

So, with the inevitable wash
of the riffling sand
beneath my feet,

I admit defeat and retreat.
We'll order pizza and
I know she loves me.

A Stone Poem

A stone is simply a fact,
but it's a curious craft
to strike the knap true.

No casual literacy
captures the elemental
like a single handprint.

So, we wait in the evening
for that last lonely echo,
listening for the dead.

But tired I forsake a lie
to sleep outside,
hoping to stay dry.

With a blanket,
the only real discomfort
is in me having my way.

But, despite an early rain
there's a reward
for being truthful.

The scent of cedar
and new mushrooms,
honest as a deep breath

This Is My Choice

To nurture an emptiness,
not a belief.

Trying to catch a fact,
this isn't that at all.

With a wink and a nod
at the chemical cabinet.

Mind expansion
can be dreadful in its intimacy.

Open wide to misinterpretation
or closed with denial.

I unwind the mystery
of my own humanity,

With ungovernable questions
and tea in the evening.

Mindfulness
plays a hollow reed.

An Unwelcome Season

In an unwelcome season,
beliefs are necessary.

Yet, we listen as if wrong
to all those winter moments

That lie within us
keeping ourselves warm.

For a leafless afternoon
or a solitary evening.

When a simple cup of tea
is a lonely ceremony.

Contemplating
beginner's mind.

And writing poetry.

Love and Hello

My wide-eyed wonder.
You who have struggled,
so long and so bitterly,
for your faith and
occasional grace.

You, who has tried to shape
the numbing minutiae of chaos
with nothing but your will.

Tell them all, or not a one,
of those who overheard us
manufacturing with our illnesses
the conflagration of our marriage.

You who heard
me talking to myself,
maddeningly laughing,
to spirits out beyond
any causal observation.

Witness to the insane man,
witless with the pain
of his own cranial lesions
And put on trial by
the magic, lantern show
of his own cerebral fluid.

And I was never quite healthy.
My own silences, critical anxiety,
and that hellish endorsement
of social necessities
has driven me
toward some niggardly vanity
in a gagging struggle
to keep my nose above water,
to keep from drowning.

Now gathering my thoughts
for a meaning,
a being of faith and honesty,
that profound synchronicity,
that I grow content.
Quietly grateful.

Taking my medication.
Sitting quietly in this tidy house
in the high desert of Oregon,
across the mountain passes.
Living with what remains
of my family after age
and foul weather
have taken the rest –

strange,
but not insane

The Bodhisattva

In the spring a bodhisattva
enters on the dew
and the world is less intent.

Nurtured by her practice
the bare limbs of an orchard
relax becoming buoyant.

So, after another thoughtless winter,
filled with all its grievances,
practice mindfulness again.

I think to trim the trees
while the lady quietly crafts
buttons of green leaf.

And after each leaf is pinned,
until the branches overflow,
a rush of cherry blossoms.

Some Memories

While some memories
remain familiar,
I am quiet.

Simple as a pebble
and a pond,
enough.

Encircled
by a tumbledown wood,
like pick-up sticks.

Practicing alchemy
with a congress of salamander
and their gentle mortality.

But accept as expected
the serious good
of serendipity.

I gather my life
clearly seeking
a curious god.

The Hermit

The hermit
as desireless

having all
his needs

no more
nor less

saying
"so"

To every nut
in the square

Neither frigid
nor frightened

The market
calculating the cost

Of the disease,
my dishabille

And the chance
of a simple recovery

Prescribes
expediency

And
loneliness

I agree

Etiquette

May memory makes whole,
as if rounded by the thumb,
the comfort in a stone.

A tenderness to be found,
in the gentle fall of leaves,
littering the graceless spaces.

Were it mine alone
the patient rain that falls
could fill all the little silences.

So, I make a pot of tea
and at the bottom of a cup
find a fine sense of irony.

Stand with the solitary man,
in the extremity of his nakedness,
mute and unobserved.

There on the brazen land
lie all his rugged miseries
and doubtless vanities.

Walking blind,
awkward, and stumbling
along all the sacred boundaries

I wonder at the cost
for what's lost is in the returning
of a simple etiquette.

Quiet

If old age
is quiet
failing health hums.

Is tinnitus
a long vowel
or a single syllable?

No elegy,
for all its brevity,
sounds quite like it.

Don't raise your voice
or speak slowly,
but be considerate.

And perhaps a prayer,
frail and dear,
to speak of death.

Except
there's still wisdom
in the old scoundrel.

Not knowing
who will sleep
and who will rest

The Zendo

It's a small tidy house,
in a nice neighborhood,
on a cool summer evening.

Grateful for a sign,
I remove my shoes
before entering.

There's a simple welcome,
quietly observed,
with tea and cookies.

But tired and anxious,
I'm self-conscious
and bothered by echoes.

Until hearing
the sound of a bell
in the hall.

I gather a mat and a pillow
and observing,
sit quietly.

The Plastic Spoon

A schizophrenic's faith,
the plastic spoon in a padded room.

Innocent enough,
yet choking on a flesh made up of flies.

A cold, dank hank of hair,
the devil's carpe' diem.

That abortion of meaning,
offending the incredulous.

With incomprehensible truths
and impenetrable insights.

Existential medicine in practice,
where the failures hemorrhage pain.

And when meaning fails,
only method remains.

Band-aid therapies,
ad nauseam.

So, give me the grace
of my own understanding.

Everyday,
Amen

Back River

Riding a bicycle
without training wheels,
My father never rode one,
I ride one still.

Our landlord, then,
owned the tavern, too,
smokey and dark,
where I took the rent.

A neighborhood woman,
in her brassiere,
watering her garden,
watches me.

And the man who owned
the ice cream truck,
I knew his son,
"Bullet."

Up too late watching
"My Three Sons."
Poor confused Ernie,
everybody liked him.

Young painted turtles
plowing their way

out of the sand,
headed for back river.

Tongue Tied

Being tongue tied
who will hear me
that isn't my guest.

How I walk steadily
and mindfully,
gaining on myself,

And finding peace.
My beliefs folding,
into tidy origami.

Politely
answer the quiet,
like a bell.

Let it be the way
my feet
hit the ground.

Windfall Apples

A hard, early frost
leaves rime in the coffee pot.
So, stir the fire up,
enough to warm a cold cup,
breakfast a windfall apple.

About in that cold,
the fields as raw as should be.
The fences are down
under the bramble and fern.
The wood coming back to true.

Awake and sleepless,
the 'possum under the boards
likes good company.
Accept a windfall apple,
eat carefully –
in quiet.

A Rose Crayon

In a world of empty words
a credible name emerges,
tabula rosa angel.

Odd child,
determinedly and
unbelievably innocent.

Who's left alone
with a sheaf of coloring paper
practicing being gifted.

Carefully turning
the crayon clouds
rose in a blue sky.

But can an artless poem,
a rain colored koan,
water the flowers?

When the homeless are dry
the hollow sound of rain
becomes profound.

And the paths of the righteous
around the grey mills
grind quietly still.

Four Days

I survived suicide
two ways:

serendipity,
serendipity,

Found
unexpectedly.

Four days,
zip-a-dee-doo-dah,

And on the fifth day,
I checked out,

Against physician's
orders,

By choice
and resolution.

We expected to die
but because of events

Beyond our control,
we survived.

And rarely attempt again,
we live

With good health

and defensive driving.

Considering suicide,
please don't.

The Final Absurdity

The tangible vote's a victory
for the ordinary prophet
and reasonably enough.

But here's to the great absurdity,
the holy grail of graciousness,
the better half of grief.

I am just a curious old man
living with a diagnosis
of Parkinson's Disease.

Worrying the anticipation,
trying not to trip over my feet
or fall out of bed.

Needing to be literal,
but not knowing less than none,
maybe somewhere in a word.

Writing what's wrong,
set on fire a new presumption,
no good intention goes unrewarded.

And whatever else changes,
with each facetious denial,
sell it to the grand old idiot.

So here I am,
from my own personal handbook,
nod if I'm not lucid.

Be Resolute

The tickets are here,
for this my serious
but quiet shadow show.

Where the wizard lisps,
whispering of himself,
abroad in the land of nod.

Hard experience
putting color in his eyes,
and a scarred eloquence.

Struggling to be outraged
at shortsighted people,
with no history of loss.

Or a reputable bunch
of discontented therapists,
with a mélange of earnest thoughts.

Schizophrenia in remission,
Post-traumatic stress hustles in,
twists my wrist until I lie.

My brother killed himself,
with all the clarity of that fact,
his anger unexpressed.

In my better moments
I wonder at this my life
and it's tenacity.

I know little brother,
brave traveler,
be resolute and go home.

Comfortable Clothes

There's a watchfulness
and a reasonable empathy
behind any equanimity.

Aware that all of the world's
aspirations are too often
just petty and mean.

There being a difference
between common reiteration
and simple reflection.

I know myself a good man,
careful of the truth,
and not ready to lie

I keep myself carefully,
but at times I'm simply
lost and unknown

So, I wear comfortable clothes,
selected each day,
for easy identification.

Sturdy black-plastic glasses,
preparing my nose,
for some odd observations.

A nice suit and neat tie,
for my church clothes,
and other odd occasions

Escorting my mother
to Sunday service,
knowing her friends.

How would I get by
without a bit of temerity?

wandering

It's a kite's fate,
turning on the wind,
mocking an urgency.

But it's an odd trigonometry
measures the immutable
with a piece of string.

Maybe it's faith
keeps it in the sky
above some friendly place.

ordinary children
collecting the winds
full of fat energy

An elementary education:
the mechanics of art,
a visceral craft.

Fellow travelers
winding up,
content in the end.

untitled

the voice is God
the word is man
I have heard
I am

The Gift

Call the gift
of simple grace
and life affirming faith,
projection.

Good enough
for this old man
to stand,
struck like a bell.

It's ringing
as inevitable
and welcome as hope
for the immaculate morning.

Summers' Mountain

Above the timberline
there's open sky,

With the sting of sunshine
and a scent of ozone.

Where glaciers still stand
in bone jarring quiet.

leaving every age
it's cirques of stone.

The snow melt in summer
still trickling down

For tenacious gardens
wild with the weather.

Rough rock zen
offers a few words

On blood pumping,
good walking days.

What a clarity
of body and mind,

Uncovering
a casual narcissism

and a heartbreaking
forgiveness.

standing back
relax and laugh

With no careless step
or scattering echo,

A marmot can still whistle
with a careless altruism.

Sunning itself
from a comfortable vantage.